FAST&FRESH

FAST&FRESH

quick recipes for busy lives

Louise Pickford
with photography by Peter Cassidy

RYLAND
PETERS
& SMALL
LONDON NEW YORK

Senior Designer Susan Downing
Commissioning Editor Elsa Petersen-Schepelern
Editor Katherine Steer
US Editor Jennifer Herman
Production Deborah Wehner
Art Director Gabriella Le Grazie
Publishing Director Alison Starling

Food Stylist Julz Beresford
Prop Stylist Helen Trent
Indexer Hilary Bird

First published in the United States in 2003
by Ryland Peters & Small, Inc.
519 Broadway, 5th Floor
New York, NY 10012
www.rylandpeters.com

10 9 8 7 6 5 4 3 2 1

Library of Congress Cataloging-in-Publication Data

Pickford, Louise.
    Fast & fresh : quick recipes for busy lives / Louise Pickford ; with
photography by Peter Cassidy.
        p. cm.
Includes index.
    ISBN 1-84172-404-1
    1. Quick and easy cookery. I. Title: Fast and fresh. II. Title.
    TX833.5 .P533 2003
    641.5'55--dc21
                                2002013769

Printed and bound in China.

Notes

All spoon measurements are level.

All eggs are large, unless otherwise specified. Uncooked or partly cooked eggs should
not be served to the very young, the very old, those with compromised immune systems,
or to pregnant women.

Author's acknowledgments
Thank you to everyone at Ryland Peters & Small for their continued support, and also to
my husband, who tastes and assesses everything I cook and still remains impartial.

CONTENTS

FAST FOOD FOR BUSY LIVES

Fast & Fresh is a recipe book for today's cook and will help you to make the best use of time when it comes to preparing a meal. Although in an ideal world it would be nice to saunter at our leisure through food markets or shop at individual suppliers, reality rarely provides us with such luxury. More usual is a quick dash to the supermarket on the way home.

Once you're in the kitchen, recipes must be fuss-free—no complicated sauces or stocks that take several hours to prepare, but just making the most of good-quality, seasonal produce. I cannot over-emphasize the importance of shopping for seasonal produce. Vegetables that were still in the ground just a few hours ago would be fantastic, but for most of us this is a bit of a pipe dream. However, buying locally grown produce is both possible and advisable—not only are they likely to taste better than those that have been picked under-ripe and transported right across the country, but also they will most likely be far cheaper too.

To me, cooking is more than purely sustenance—it is also a love and passion for creating flavors that delight and dishes that satisfy. It is the pleasure of sitting down with friends or family, sharing thoughts and anecdotes, or just enjoying the food and company with a glass of wine. Cooking should be fun, not a chore.

Because most of us want a quick fix at the end of a busy day, we often opt for fast or convenience foods that will fill the gap—but do these ever truly satisfy us? What if you could shop, prepare, and cook a delicious meal in the time it takes to order and collect that takeout? With *Fast & Fresh* you can.

Sometimes, especially when I'm in a hurry, I might skip the appetizer altogether and just concentrate on the entrée—and a dessert, of course.

Other times, I make a quick antipasti with my favorite things from the deli counter—perhaps prosciutto, salami, and other cold cuts—plus a dish of olives, or toast and dips.

A simple salad also makes a great appetizer—just crisp green leaves and a vinaigrette, either plain or with blue cheese added. Or something exotic, such as the pea shoots with wasabi-flavored mayonnaise on page 14. Or use the same wasabi mayonnaise as a dip for some raw fresh vegetables or crudités.

Often, however, I think that appetizers are the most exciting part of a meal. You can turn them into a whole meal if you like—I sometimes make a selection of dishes, so people can dip in, as you do with mezze or tapas. This is a fun way to eat and although you may need a little more time to prepare a selection of dishes, there is little else to do later other than enjoy the meal.

APPETIZERS

Thai fish, shrimp, or crab cakes are quick and easy to make—perfect as an appetizer, or as a spicy snack with cocktails. If you have time, marinate the shrimp mixture for 30 minutes or so. I keep a few bottles of chile jam in the pantry, but you can use a prepared chile sauce if you prefer.

THAI SHRIMP CAKES

WITH CHILE JAM

To make the chile jam, put the tomatoes, chiles, and garlic in a food processor and purée until smooth. Transfer to a saucepan, add the ginger, soy sauce, sugar, vinegar, and salt, and bring to a boil. Cook for 30–35 minutes, stirring occasionally until thick and glossy.

Warm the jars in a low oven, pour in the thickened jam, and let cool completely. Seal and store in the refrigerator.

To make the shrimp cakes, put the shrimp into a food processor and blend to a purée. Add the lime leaves, scallions, cilantro, egg, fish sauce, and rice flour, blend briefly, and transfer to a bowl. Using damp hands, shape the mixture into 24 patties, 2 inches diameter.

Pour $1/2$-inch depth of the oil in a skillet, heat for 1 minute over medium heat, then add the cakes, spaced apart. Sauté in batches for 2 minutes on each side until golden brown. Remove and drain on paper towels and keep them warm in a low oven while you cook the remainder. Serve with chile jam or sweet chile sauce.

1 lb. uncooked, shelled and deveined shrimp

4 lime leaves, very finely chopped, or grated zest of 1 lime

4 scallions, finely chopped

2 tablespoons chopped fresh cilantro

1 egg

1 tablespoon Thai fish sauce

$1/3$ cup rice flour or cornstarch

peanut or safflower oil, for frying

chile jam (below) or
sweet chile sauce, to serve

chile jam

1 lb. ripe tomatoes, coarsely chopped

3–4 red chiles, coarsely chopped

2 garlic cloves, chopped

1 teaspoon grated fresh ginger

2 tablespoons light soy sauce

$1 1/4$ cups palm sugar or brown sugar

$1/2$ cup white wine vinegar

$1/2$ teaspoon sea salt

*2 preserving jars, about
1 cup each, sterilized*

serves 6 (makes 24 cakes)

This spicy eggplant dip is like Middle Eastern baba ganoush eggplant purée, but uses yogurt instead of tahini. The eggplant should be charred well to achieve the best smoky flavor.

CHAR-GRILLED EGGPLANT DIP

Cut the eggplant lengthwise into thin slices, about 1/8 inch. Put the oil in a small bowl, add the cumin, salt, and pepper, mix well, then brush all over the eggplant.

Cook on a preheated stove-top grill pan or under a hot broiler for 3–4 minutes on each side until charred and tender. Let cool, then chop finely.

Put the yogurt in a bowl, then stir in the eggplant, scallions, and lemon juice. Taste and adjust the seasoning with salt and pepper. Serve in bowls or on plates, with toasted pita bread for dipping.

1 large eggplant

2 tablespoons extra virgin olive oil

1 teaspoon ground cumin

1 cup plain yogurt

2 scallions, finely chopped

1 tablespoon freshly squeezed lemon juice

sea salt and freshly ground black pepper

toasted pita bread, to serve

serves 6

If you can find Greek tzatziki dip, use this instead of the chive cheese. This topping can also be used as a sandwich filling.

SMOKED SALMON BRUSCHETTA
WITH ARUGULA AND CHIVE CHEESE

Toast the bread on a preheated stove-top grill pan or under a hot broiler. While still hot, rub all over with the garlic and sprinkle with oil. Mix the cream cheese and chives, add a large spoonful to each slice, then pile on the salmon and arugula. Season with pepper and serve sprinkled with a little extra oil.

4 thick slices of sourdough bread

1 large garlic clove, halved

2 tablespoons extra virgin olive oil, plus extra to serve

8 oz. cream cheese

2 tablespoons chopped fresh chives

8 oz. smoked salmon slices

a handful of arugula

freshly ground black pepper

serves 6

HOMEMADE HERB CHEESE

Put all the ingredients in a bowl and stir well. Line a second bowl with a large piece of cheesecloth and spoon in the yogurt mixture. Pull up the ends of the cheesecloth to form a bag and tie tightly with kitchen twine.

Hang the bag over the bowl so the liquid can drain from the yogurt. Leave in the refrigerator overnight. Unwrap the bag and transfer the cheese to a serving bowl. Serve with whole wheat or soda bread.

1¾ cups plain yogurt

¼ cup heavy cream

1 garlic clove, crushed

3 tablespoons chopped fresh basil

3 tablespoons chopped mixed fresh herbs, including dill, marjoram, parsley, and thyme leaves

sea salt and freshly ground black pepper

whole wheat or soda bread (page 112)

a piece of cheesecloth, 12 inches square

serves 4–6

Pea shoots are the tendrils and baby leaves of snowpeas. You often see them in Chinese and Southeast Asian markets, but if you can't find any, use watercress instead. I will give a delicious peppery flavor, which mirrors the fiery spice of wasabi.

PEA SHOOT SALAD
WITH WASABI MAYONNAISE

Heat 2 inches of oil in deep saucepan to 350°F on a candy thermometer (or a cube of bread crisps and browns in 30 seconds). Break the noodles into 2-inch lengths and add to the oil in 4 batches (be careful because the fat will foam up as the noodles are added). Fry for 1–2 minutes until crisp. Drain on paper towels and sprinkle with salt.

Mix the mayonnaise, wasabi, and vinegar in a bowl. Add the pea shoots or watercress and radishes and toss until evenly coated. Top with the noodles and serve at once.

4 oz. dried Chinese egg noodles, soaked and drained according to the directions on the package

8 oz. pea shoots or watercress

4 oz. radishes, sliced and cut into strips

sea salt

peanut or safflower oil, for deep-frying

wasabi mayonnaise dressing

1 recipe Mayonnaise (page 142)

1 tablespoon wasabi paste

2 tablespoons rice wine vinegar

serves 4

Yogurt-crusted chicken threaded onto skewers makes ideal finger food for buffets and cocktail parties. The yogurt tenderizes the chicken and helps the lemon soak into the meat. For the best flavor, cook them on an outdoor grill— the yogurt becomes delicious and slightly crunchy.

CHICKEN AND LEMON SKEWERS

Cut the chicken lengthwise into $\frac{1}{8}$-inch strips and put in a shallow ceramic dish.

Put all the marinade ingredients in a bowl, stir well, and pour over the chicken. Turn to coat, cover, and let marinate in the refrigerator overnight.

The next day, thread the chicken onto the soaked bamboo skewers, zig-zagging the meat back and forth as you go.

Cook on a preheated outdoor grill or under a hot broiler for 3–4 minutes on each side until charred and tender. Let cool slightly before serving.

1 lb. skinless, boneless chicken breasts

marinade

1 cup plain yogurt

2 tablespoons extra virgin olive oil

2 garlic cloves, crushed

grated zest and freshly squeezed juice of 1 unwaxed lemon

1–2 teaspoons ground chiles

1 tablespoon chopped fresh cilantro

sea salt and freshly ground black pepper

12 bamboo skewers, soaked in cold water for 30 minutes

serves 4

VEGETARIAN AND SIDES

This chapter is about cooking vegetables as well as cooking vegetarian food.

Buying seasonal produce will reap great rewards. Though most of us aren't fortunate enough to have a vegetable garden, there are often farmers' or organic markets which offer the best chance of buying ingredients harvested within hours of purchase.

If you have good-quality produce, the rest is easy—add a single herb or spice to compliment a particular vegetable and make a side dish that tastes wonderful and will go well with a whole range of meat and fish.

Living with a non-meat-eater means I eat very little meat myself and, although we both eat fish, vegetable dishes form the basis of our diet. This chapter is great for vegetarians looking for quick and simple recipes, but I hope it will also surprise and inspire many who feel a meat-free meal can be a bit dull.

I often hear it said that vegetarian food is all well and good if you have plenty of time, but that's no help if you're in hurry. Let me dispel that myth and prove it is just as quick and easy to make a meat-free meal as any other.

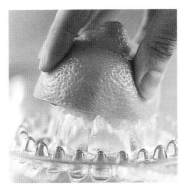

Tabbouleh, the fresh parsley salad from Lebanon, is based on bulghur wheat. This one is made with couscous, the fine Moroccan pasta, now available in an instant version—you just soak it in water or stock for 10 minutes or so.

FRAGRANT HERB COUSCOUS SALAD

To make the fragrant garlic oil, peel the cloves and put them in a saucepan. Add the bay leaves and oil and heat gently for 15 minutes until the garlic has softened. Don't let the garlic brown. Let cool, remove and mash the garlic cloves, then return them to the oil. Refrigerate until required. Use 1¼ cups for this recipe and reserve the remainder.

Put the couscous in a bowl, add water to cover by 2 inches and let soak for 10 minutes.

Drain the soaked couscous, shaking the strainer well to remove any excess water. Transfer to a bowl, add the fragrant garlic oil, lemon juice, chopped basil, cilantro, mint and parsley. Season with salt and pepper, then set aside to develop the flavors until ready to serve. Serve with halved lemons, if using.

1½ cups couscous

freshly squeezed juice of 1 lemon

2 tablespoons chopped fresh basil

2 tablespoons chopped fresh cilantro

2 tablespoons chopped fresh mint

2 tablespoons chopped fresh parsley

sea salt and freshly ground black pepper

2 lemons, halved, to serve (optional)

fragrant garlic oil

1 whole head of garlic, cloves separated

2 bay leaves

2¾ cups extra virgin olive oil

serves 4

1 tablespoon toasted sesame oil

1 onion, sliced

8 oz. string beans

12 oz. deep-fried tofu, sliced

2 tablespoons sweet chile sauce

a handful basil leaves, preferably Thai

2 tablespoons sesame seeds,
toasted in a dry skillet

sauce

1¾ cups coconut milk

1½ cups Vegetable Stock (page 143)

2 stalks of lemongrass, sliced crosswise

1 tablespoon Thai fish sauce

8 lime leaves, sliced, or grated lime zest

2 garlic cloves, chopped

1 inch fresh ginger, peeled and grated

serves 4

Deep-fried tofu cakes are available from Asian markets or natural food stores where they can be found in the refrigerator. You can substitute regular firm tofu, cut into cubes instead.

STIR-FRIED TOFU
WITH CHILE COCONUT SAUCE

Put all the sauce ingredients in a saucepan, bring to a boil, and simmer for 20 minutes until reduced by half. Strain the sauce and reserve.

Cut the beans into 2-inch lengths. Heat the oil in a wok or skillet and stir-fry the onions and beans for 1 minute, add the tofu cakes, and stir-fry for a further 1 minute. Add the coconut sauce, sweet chile sauce, and basil leaves and heat through. Serve sprinkled with the sesame seeds.

PEA AND MINT SOUP

Melt the butter in a saucepan, add the leeks, potatoes, and garlic, and sauté for 10 minutes. Add the peas, stock, mint sprigs, and a little salt and pepper and bring to a boil. Cover and simmer for 20 minutes. Discard the mint sprigs.

Transfer the soup to a blender, add the chopped mint, then purée until very smooth. Return to the pan, season to taste, and heat through. Serve the soup topped with a spoonful of sour cream and a generous grinding of black pepper.

4 tablespoons unsalted butter

2 leeks, trimmed, split, well washed, then chopped

1 large baking potatoes, chopped, 8 oz.

1 garlic clove, crushed

1½ lb. fresh or frozen peas

1 quart Chicken or Vegetable Stock (page 143)

2 tablespoons chopped fresh mint, plus 2 sprigs

sea salt and freshly ground black pepper

sour cream or crème fraîche, to serve

serves 6

We're into fast cooking, so this is a cheat's curry because I have used a ready-made curry paste. Serve with basmati rice.

QUICK VEGETABLE CURRY

Heat the oil in a saucepan and sauté the onion, garlic, ginger, curry paste, and cinnamon for 5 minutes. Add the potatoes, tomatoes, stock, tomato purée, salt, and pepper. Bring to a boil, cover, and simmer gently for 20 minutes.

Add the mushrooms, peas, ground almonds, and cilantro to the pan and cook for a further 10 minutes. Taste and adjust the seasoning with salt and pepper, then serve.

Note If you can't find ground almonds, use blanched almonds and grind them with a mortar and pestle or small blender.

3 tablespoons peanut or safflower oil

1 onion, sliced

2 garlic cloves, chopped

1 inch fresh ginger, peeled and grated

1 tablespoon hot red curry paste

1 teaspoon ground cinnamon

1 lb. baking potatoes, cut into cubes

14 oz. canned chopped tomatoes

1¼ cups Vegetable Stock (page 143)

1 tablespoon tomato purée

8 oz. button mushrooms, halved

8 oz. frozen peas

⅓ cup finely ground almonds

2 tablespoons chopped fresh cilantro

sea salt and freshly ground black pepper

serves 4

2 tablespoons peanut oil

1 tablespoon toasted sesame oil

2 garlic cloves, sliced

1 red chile, seeded and sliced

2 lb. Savoy cabbage, finely shredded

1 tablespoon chopped fresh cilantro

freshly squeezed juice of ½ lemon

⅓ cup dry-roasted peanuts

2 tablespoons sesame seeds, toasted

sea salt and ground Szechuan pepper

serves 4

STIR-FRIED SESAME CABBAGE

Heat the two oils together in a wok or large, deep skillet, add the garlic and chile, and stir-fry over high heat for 30 seconds.

Add the cabbage and stir-fry for a further 2–3 minutes until golden and the cabbage is starting to soften.

Add the cilantro, lemon juice, peanuts, sesame seeds, salt, and pepper, stir well, and transfer to a warmed dish. Serve at once.

Basil oil is particularly good sprinkled onto this simple tart, but you can use ordinary olive oil. Preheating the baking sheet will make the base of the tart beautifully crisp.

SIMPLE TOMATO AND OLIVE TART
WITH PARMESAN

To make the basil oil, blanch the leaves very briefly in boiling water, drain, and dry thoroughly with paper towels. Put in a blender, add the oil and salt, and blend until very smooth. Pour the oil through a fine strainer, or one lined with cheesecloth. Keep in the refrigerator but return to room temperature before using.

Preheat the oven to 425°F and put a baking tray on the middle shelf.

Roll out the dough on a lightly floured surface to form a rectangle, 10 x 12 inches. Trim the edges and transfer the dough to a second baking tray. Using the blade of a sharp knife, gently tap the edges several times (this will help the dough rise and the edges separate) and prick all over with a fork.

Put the tomatoes, olives, basil oil, salt, and pepper in a bowl and mix lightly. Spoon the mixture over the dough and carefully slide the tart directly onto the preheated baking tray. Bake for 12–15 minutes until risen and golden.

Remove from the oven and sprinkle with the Parmesan. Cut into quarters and serve hot with a handful of arugula.

12 oz. ready-made puff pastry dough, thawed if frozen

4 oz. red cherry tomatoes, halved

8 oz. yellow cherry tomatoes, halved

½ cup semi-dried or sun-dried tomatoes, halved

½ cup black olives, such as Niçoise or Kalamata, pitted and halved

2 tablespoons basil oil (below)

1 oz. freshly grated Parmesan cheese, about ⅓ cup

sea salt and freshly ground black pepper

a handful of arugula, to serve

basil oil

1 oz. fresh basil leaves, about 1 cup

⅔ cup extra virgin olive oil

a pinch of sea salt

2 baking trays

serves 4

Red lentils are widely used in Indian cooking to make dhaal—
a sauce to serve with rice. They are healthy, nutritious, and
delicious. Serve this dish as part of an Indian meal.

CURRIED RED LENTILS

Put the onion, garlic, and ginger in a food processor and blend to form a fairly smooth purée. Heat the butter in a saucepan, add the purée, tomatoes, and spices, and sauté gently for about 5 minutes.

Add the lentils, stock, lemon juice, salt, and pepper, bring to a boil, cover, and simmer over low heat for about 20 minutes until the lentils have thickened.

Taste and adjust the seasoning with salt and pepper, then serve topped with a few fried curry leaves, if using.

1 onion, chopped

2 garlic cloves, chopped

1 inch fresh ginger, peeled and grated

4 tablespoons unsalted butter

12 oz. tomatoes, chopped

1 tablespoon curry powder

1 teaspoon ground turmeric

½ teaspoon ground cinnamon

12 oz. red lentils, about 1¾ cups

4 cups Vegetable Stock (page 143), or good quality store-bought stock

freshly squeezed juice of ½ lemon

sea salt and freshly ground black pepper

2–3 sprigs of fresh or frozen curry leaves, fried for a few seconds in 2 tablespoons unsalted butter (optional)

serves 6

Although it may sound unusual, chocolate is the secret ingredient of this Mexican-inspired dish. It adds a wonderfully rich, intense flavor to the vegetables. Serve with rice, or the Chile Cornbread on page 115.

QUICK VEGETARIAN MOLE

Heat the oil in a saucepan and sauté the onion, pepper, garlic, and spices for 5 minutes. Add the sweet potatoes, tomatoes, beans, chile sauce, and 1¼ cups water and bring to a boil. Cover and simmer over gentle heat for 30 minutes.

Stir in the chocolate and fresh cilantro and cook for a final 5 minutes. Taste and adjust the seasoning with salt and pepper, then serve.

2 tablespoons peanut or safflower oil

1 red onion, chopped

1 large red bell pepper, seeded and chopped

2 garlic cloves

2 teaspoons ground coriander

1 teaspoon ground cumin

½ teaspoon ground cinnamon

1 lb. sweet potatoes, cut into cubes

1 lb. canned chopped tomatoes, about 2 cups

1 lb. canned red kidney beans, rinsed and drained, about 2 cups

1–2 teaspoons sweet chile sauce

1 oz. dark chocolate, grated

2 tablespoons chopped fresh cilantro

sea salt and freshly ground black pepper

serves 4

2 lb. mixed baby vegetables, trimmed, washed, and peeled as necessary

black bean dressing

2 tablespoons canned black beans, drained, rinsed, and drained again

1 garlic clove, crushed

1 teaspoon grated fresh ginger

1 tablespoon rice wine vinegar

1 tablespoon light soy sauce

½ cup peanut oil

serves 6

STEAMED BABY VEGETABLES
WITH BLACK BEAN DRESSING

To make the dressing, put the beans in a bowl, add 3 tablespoons cold water, mash lightly with a fork, then stir in the garlic, ginger, vinegar, soy sauce, and peanut oil.

Steam the vegetables over a saucepan of simmering water, starting with the largest and adding the rest depending on size, until the vegetables are tender. Transfer to a large bowl and pass the dressing around in a separate bowl so guests can help themselves.

This recipe is based on a favorite Greek dish—*gigantes* or "big beans." The Quick Tomato Sauce can be made ahead.

2 tablespoons extra virgin olive oil

1 onion, chopped

½ teaspoon hot red pepper flakes

1¾ lb. canned lima beans, rinsed and drained, about 5 cups

1 recipe Quick Tomato Sauce (page 142)

sea salt and freshly ground black pepper

to serve

toast

freshly grated Parmesan cheese

serves 4

LIMA BEANS
WITH QUICK TOMATO SAUCE

Heat the oil in a saucepan and gently sauté the onion and hot red pepper flakes for 10 minutes until softened but not golden.

Add the beans, stir once, then add the quick tomato sauce. Bring to a boil, cover with a lid, and simmer gently for about 20 minutes. Taste and adjust the seasoning with salt and pepper and serve piled onto toast with a sprinkling of freshly grated Parmesan.

WHITE BEAN SOUP
WITH OLIVE GREMOLATA

Heat the oil in a saucepan and sauté the onion, garlic, and sage for 5 minutes until golden. Add the potatoes and beans, stir well, then add the stock, bay leaves, salt, and pepper.

Bring to a boil, cover, and simmer gently for 20 minutes until the potatoes are tender. Transfer half the soup to a blender and blend until smooth. Return to the pan, adjust the seasoning, and heat through.

Meanwhile, to make the gremolata, finely chop the olives and mix with lemon zest and parsley. Serve the soup in warm bowls topped with the gremolata.

¼ cup extra virgin olive oil

1 large onion, chopped

2 garlic cloves, crushed

1 tablespoon chopped fresh sage

1 lb. baking potatoes, cut into cubes

1¾ lb. canned white beans, drained, about 5 cups

1 quart Vegetable Stock (page 143)

2 bay leaves

1 cup pitted black olives, such as Niçoise

grated zest of 1 unwaxed lemon

2 tablespoons chopped fresh parsley

sea salt and freshly ground black pepper

serves 6

EGGSANDCHEESE

Eggs and dairy products are the victims of a bad press and constantly changing reputations. One minute they're bad for people watching their weight—the next, they're good.

A balanced diet is vital for a healthy body, and eggs and dairy products are excellent sources of protein and calcium which help build strong bones in the young and reduce the chances of osteoporosis in later life. They taste good and are good for you—especially for people who don't eat meat.

The other great thing about egg and cheese dishes is they are usually very quick to make. Take an omelet or scrambled eggs, for instance—ready in minutes. Cheese on toast? A perfect late-night instant snack. I love dishes like these. I find them comforting and familiar, perhaps because they remind me of the food my mother used to cook for me when I was a kid.

Smoked salmon and baked eggs make the perfect breakfast treat—and take no time at all. In fact, if you're having people over on the weekend for brunch, there can be no quicker, easier, or more elegant dish to serve as part of the spread.

BAKED EGGS
WITH SMOKED SALMON AND CHIVES

Divide the smoked salmon and chives between the 4 buttered ramekins. Make a small indent in the salmon with the back of a spoon and break an egg in the hollow, sprinkle with a little pepper, and spoon the cream over the top.

Put the ramekins in a roasting pan and half-fill the pan with boiling water. Bake in a preheated oven at 350°F for 10–15 minutes until the eggs have just set. Remove from the oven, let cool for a few minutes, then serve with toast.

8 oz. smoked salmon slices, chopped

1 tablespoon chopped fresh chives

4 eggs

¼ cup heavy cream

sea salt and freshly ground black pepper

toast, to serve

4 ramekins, 1 cup each, well buttered

serves 4

This recipe serves two because it's not easy to cook more than this quantity at once. Regular or portobello mushrooms are fine, but if you can find wild mushrooms such as girolle or chanterelle, then you are in for a real treat.

SCRAMBLED EGGS
WITH MUSHROOMS

Wipe the mushrooms with a damp cloth and cut into thick slices. Put the eggs in a bowl, add salt and pepper, and beat until blended.

Melt 3 tablespoons of the butter in a large skillet. As soon as it stops foaming, add the mushrooms, thyme, salt, and pepper. Sauté over medium heat until lightly browned and the juices are starting to run.

Push the mushrooms to one side of the pan, add the remaining butter, then pour in the beaten eggs, stirring with a fork until almost set.

Gradually stir in the mushrooms from the sides of the pan, cook a moment longer, and spoon onto toast. Sprinkle with chopped parsley, if using, and serve with toast.

8 oz. portobello mushrooms, or mixed wild mushrooms

6 eggs

4 tablespoons unsalted butter

2 teaspoons chopped fresh thyme leaves

sea salt and freshly ground black pepper

to serve

chopped fresh parsley (optional)

toast

sautéed mushrooms (optional)

serves 2

Perfectly set eggs spiked with the fragrance of mixed fresh herbs makes a perfect supper dish and I love to dot the frittata with a little ricotta just before the top is broiled. Cut into small squares, frittata makes great finger food.

FRITTATA

WITH FRESH HERBS AND RICOTTA

Put the eggs in a bowl, add the herbs, celery salt, if using, and a good sprinkling of salt and pepper. Beat with a fork.

Preheat the broiler. Heat the oil in a non-stick skillet until hot, then add the egg mixture. Cook over medium heat for 5–6 minutes until almost set. Dot the ricotta over the top and cook under a hot broiler until the surface is set and browned.

Let cool slightly, then cut in wedges, and serve warm.

6 eggs

a large handful of chopped mixed fresh herbs, such as basil, chervil, chives, marjoram, mint, and/or parsley

1 teaspoon celery salt (optional)

2 tablespoons extra virgin olive oil

4 oz. fresh ricotta cheese, about ½ cup, crumbled into big pieces

sea salt and freshly ground black pepper

serves 4

BAKED CHEVRE

Put the slices of chèvre onto the prepared baking tray, sprinkle with a little oil, dot with thyme leaves, and season with pepper. Bake in a preheated oven at 400°F for 10–12 minutes until just starting to ooze and run.

Meanwhile, toast the sourdough and rub it with the garlic. When the cheese is ready, spread it onto the toasted, garlicky sourdough and serve with a green salad.

4 thick slices of goat cheese with rind (Bûcheron), 2 oz. per serving

extra virgin olive oil, for sprinkling

1 tablespoon chopped fresh thyme

freshly ground black pepper

to serve

4 slices of sourdough bread

1–2 garlic cloves, halved

green salad

a baking tray, lined with foil

serves 4

Simple and delicious, this recipe can be served as an appetizer or as a snack with a green salad. Use a creamy goat cheese with a rind that will soften nicely without melting.

BROILED ASPARAGUS
WITH GOAT CHEESE AND HERB OIL

Preheat the broiler. Trim the asparagus spears and rub or brush with a little of the Thyme Oil, sprinkle with salt and pepper, and cook under a hot broiler for 4–5 minutes, turning half-way through until charred and tender.

Arrange on plates and top each one with a slice of the cheese, return to the broiler very briefly until the cheese is softened but not browned. Sprinkle with more Thyme Oil and serve with crusty bread.

1 lb. asparagus spears

1 tablespoon Thyme Oil (page 140), plus extra to serve

4 oz. goat cheese, sliced

sea salt and freshly ground black pepper

baguette, to serve

serves 4

My favorite thing when I get back late from the movies or a show—quick, delicious, and washing-up-free. It tastes great with almost any chutney or relish. Be ready to provide seconds.

CHEESE ON TOAST

Toast the bread under the broiler on one side only. Grate the cheese onto the untoasted side of the bread (if using very soft cheese, slice it instead). Add a few drops of Worcestershire sauce, if using, and broil for 2–3 minutes until melted and bubbling.

Serve on a platter with the bottle of pickles, relish, or chutney and a spoon so that guests can help themselves.

2 thick slices of white bread

4 oz. cheese, such as Cheddar, a soft creamy goat cheese, or Brie

a few drops of Worcestershire sauce (optional)

pickles, relish, or chutney, to serve

serves 2

Make this dish only when top-quality fresh figs are in season. Otherwise use peaches, nectarines, or melon wedges.

FIGS WITH MARINATED FETA

Put the garlic, chile, lemon zest, cumin, mint, and oil in a bowl, add the feta, and toss gently. Set aside to marinate for at least 30 minutes (this can be done the night before).

Slice the figs in half and serve on the toasted bread with the feta and marinade juices, then serve sprinkled with a little Reduced Balsamic Vinegar.

1 garlic clove, crushed

1 red chile, seeded and chopped

grated zest of 1 unwaxed lemon

1/2 teaspoon ground cumin

1 tablespoon chopped fresh mint

1/3 cup extra virgin olive oil

8 oz. feta cheese, crumbled

4–6 large ripe figs

4 slices toasted sourdough bread

cracked black pepper

Reduced Balsamic Vinegar, to serve (page 141)

serves 4

Served warm, these soufflés are a favorite of mine because I don't have to panic getting them to the table before they sink! Make sure you butter the ramekin dishes very well so that you can get the soufflés out.

WARM GOAT CHEESE SOUFFLES

Melt the butter in a saucepan, add the flour, and cook over low heat for 30 seconds. Remove the pan from the heat and gradually stir in the milk until smooth. Return to the heat and stir constantly until the mixture thickens. Cook for 1 minute.

Cool slightly and beat in the cheese, egg yolks, herbs, salt, and pepper. Put the egg whites in a bowl and beat until soft peaks form. Fold the egg whites into the cheese mixture.

Spoon the mixture into the ramekins and bake in a preheated oven 400°F for 15–18 minutes until risen and golden on top. Remove from the oven and let cool for about 15 minutes.

Using a spatula, work round the edges of the soufflés and turn them out onto plates. Serve with arugula salad.

2 tablespoons unsalted butter

2 tablespoons all-purpose flour

1 cup milk

4 oz. soft goat cheese

3 eggs, separated

2 tablespoons chopped fresh mixed herbs, such as basil, chives, mint, and tarragon

sea salt and freshly ground black pepper

arugula salad, to serve

6 ramekins, 1 cup each, well buttered

serves 6

FISHANDSEAFOOD

Since moving to Australia, I have learned a great deal about the freshness of seafood, something that is unfortunately not always available in other countries.

However, top-quality seafood can be found, and it is usually just a case of seeking out a good supplier. Supermarkets are improving all the time and will only continue to do so if you, the customer, demand quality.

Don't be afraid to talk to your fishsellers, ask them questions—most are only too glad to share their knowledge.

When shopping for shellfish, avoid any that are sitting in water, and when buying fish, look for bright eyes and shiny skin. They should smell of the sea (not at all fishy).

Simplicity is the name of the game when you're cooking seafood. Let the flavors speak for themselves by serving it quickly cooked and simply dressed—perhaps just with a drizzle of oil and fragrant chopped herbs or a pat of spiced butter.

Shrimp make the fastest, freshest, most impressive dish you can imagine. If you can't find uncooked shrimp, use precooked ones—just sprinkle them with the chile oil and lemon juice and serve with the cool and refreshing pesto. Now, how complicated can that be!

SHRIMP WITH CHILE OIL
AND PISTACHIO AND MINT PESTO

To make the pesto, put the pistachios, mint, garlic, and scallions in a food processor and grind coarsely. Add the oil and purée until fairly smooth and green. Stir in the vinegar and season to taste. Set aside while you prepare the shrimp, or store in the refrigerator for up to 5 days.

Put the shrimp in a shallow dish and sprinkle with the Chile Oil, salt, and pepper. Cover and let marinate for at least 30 minutes or longer, if possible.

When ready to serve, thread the shrimp onto skewers and cook on a preheated outdoor grill or stove-top grill pan, or under a hot broiler, for about 2 minutes on each side until charred and tender—the flesh should be just opaque. Do not overcook or the shrimp will be tough.

Put on separate plates or a large platter, sprinkle with fresh lemon juice, and serve with the pesto and crusty bread to mop up the juices.

24 large uncooked shrimp, shelled and deveined

1/4 cup Chile Oil (page 140)

freshly squeezed juice of 1 lemon

pistachio and mint pesto

2 oz. shelled pistachios, about 1/3 cup

a bunch of mint

1 garlic clove, crushed

2 scallions, chopped

1/2 cup extra virgin olive oil

1 tablespoon white wine vinegar

sea salt and freshly ground black pepper

to serve

1 lemon, cut into wedges

crusty bread

serves 4

Try to find small clams—I think they are sweeter and more tender than the larger varieties. This recipe will serve four as an appetizer, but you can serve it with other Asian dishes plus rice and noodles for an impressive banquet.

DRUNKEN CLAMS

Tap each clam lightly on the work surface and discard any that won't close. Put the clams in a saucepan, add the stock, rice wine, garlic, ginger, scallions, and chile. Grind Szechuan pepper over the top and bring to the boil. Cover with a lid and let steam for 3–4 minutes until all the shells have opened.

Discard any unopened clams and transfer the rest to warmed bowls. Pour the stock through a fine strainer, pour over the clams, then serve.

4 lb. fresh clams, well scrubbed

2/3 cup Fish or Vegetable Stock (page 143)

1/2 cup Shaohsing (sweetened Chinese rice wine) or sweet sherry

4 garlic cloves, sliced

1 inch fresh ginger, peeled and sliced

6 scallions, sliced

1 red chile, seeded and sliced

Szechuan pepper or black pepper

serves 4

A simple dish with lovely flavors—when you serve lobster, the effect is instantly luxurious and "special occasion." Who would ever know this dish was so simple to prepare? Slice the fennel as finely as possible, using a mandoline if you have one. If not, it's worthwhile investing in one so you can cut vegetables very thinly into slices or matchsticks. Inexpensive, but effective, plastic Japanese mandolines are available from kitchen stores.

LOBSTER AND FENNEL SALAD

Trim off and discard the tough outer layer of fennel, then chop and reserve the fronds. Cut the bulb in half, then cut crosswise into very thin slices. Put in a bowl, add the lemon juice, oil, fennel fronds, salt, and pepper, toss well, then marinate for 15 minutes.

Cut the lobsters in half and lift the tail flesh out of the shell. Crack the claws with a small hammer or crab crackers and carefully remove all the meat.

Put a layer of shaved fennel salad on each plate, top with the lobster, and serve with a spoonful of mayonnaise.

1 large bulb of fennel

freshly squeezed juice of $1/2$ lemon

$1/4$ cup extra virgin olive oil

4 small cooked lobsters, about 1 lb. each, or 2 large ones

1 recipe Mayonnaise (page 142)

sea salt and freshly ground black pepper

serves 4

The squid will curl up as they cook, so I use a pair of tongs to open them out again and press flat. You could also put a heatproof plate on top to keep them that way. Take care not to overcook squid or it will be tough.

SEARED SQUID
WITH LEMON AND CILANTRO DRESSING

To make the dressing, put the ingredients in a screw-top bottle, shake well, and use as required. If storing in the refrigerator, omit the cilantro, and add just before use.

Cut the squid bodies in half and open out flat. Brush with the olive oil and season with salt and pepper.

Heat a stove-top grill pan for 5 minutes until very hot. Add the squid bodies and tentacles and cook for 1 minute on each side until charred and tender. Transfer to a board and cut the squid into thick slices.

Put the dressing in a bowl, add the squid, and toss well. Serve with a few baby spinach leaves and extra black pepper.

Note Squid is very easy to clean. Pull out the tentacles (the insides should come with them). Cut off the tentacles and discard the insides. Rinse out the bodies, pulling out the stiff transparent quill, like a little wand of plastic. Use the bodies and tentacles. That's it.

4 medium squid, cleaned, about 1½ lb.

1 tablespoon extra virgin olive oil

sea salt and freshly ground black pepper

baby spinach leaves, to serve

lemon and cilantro dressing

⅓ cup peanut oil

1 tablespoon toasted sesame oil

freshly squeezed juice of 1 lemon

2 tablespoons sweet soy sauce, (Indonesian *ketchap manis*), or regular soy sauce with ½ teaspoon sugar added

2 tablespoons chopped fresh cilantro

1 garlic clove, crushed

serves 4

Scallops, with their sweet flesh and subtle hint of the sea, are a real treat. Truffle oil, though expensive, is used sparingly and transforms this dish into something special. If you don't have any truffle oil, use either Thyme Oil (page 140) or Fragrant Garlic Oil (page 21).

SEARED SCALLOPS
WITH CRUSHED POTATOES

Cook the potatoes in a saucepan of lightly salted, boiling water until just tender. Drain well and return to the pan. Lightly crush them with a fork leaving them still a little chunky. Add the olive oil, olives, parsley, and a few drops of truffle oil, if using. Season with salt and pepper and stir well.

Put the scallops in a bowl, add the olive oil, salt, and pepper. Sear the scallops on a preheated stove-top grill pan for 1 minute on each side (don't overcook or they will be tough). Remove to a plate and let them rest briefly.

Put a pile of crushed potatoes onto each plate, put the scallops on top, and sprinkle with a few extra drops of truffle oil, if using.

12 large sea scallops

1 tablespoon extra virgin olive oil

sea salt and freshly ground black pepper

crushed potatoes

1 lb. new potatoes, peeled

1 tablespoon extra virgin olive oil

1/4 cup pitted black olives, chopped

1 tablespoon chopped
fresh flat-leaf parsley

a few drops of truffle oil (optional)

sea salt and freshly ground black pepper

serves 4

Peppery radish and fresh mint yogurt tempers the heat from the spice-coated fish, though if you don't like very spicy food, you could leave out the chili powder and rely on the freshly ground black pepper and crunchy radishes alone. Serve crusty bread on the side to mop up the juices.

BLACKENED MONKFISH
WITH RADISH AND MINT YOGURT

Mix all the spice mix ingredients together and sprinkle on a plate. Roll the fish in the spice mix until well coated.

Melt the butter and oil in a nonstick skillet, then as soon as it stops foaming, add the fish. Sauté over medium heat for 4 minutes on each side, until browned all over. Transfer to a warm oven and let rest for 5 minutes.

Put the yogurt in a bowl, add the radishes, cucumber, mint, garlic, salt, and pepper, and stir well. Serve with the browned fish.

4 fillets monkfish or cod, 8 oz. each, skinned

4 tablespoons unsalted butter

1 tablespoon peanut oil

1 cup plain yogurt

4 radishes, cut into matchstick strips, plus extra to serve

1/2 cucumber, peeled, seeded, and cut into matchstick strips

1 tablespoon chopped fresh mint

1 garlic clove, crushed

sea salt and freshly ground black pepper

spice mix

2 tablespoons chopped fresh thyme leaves

1 tablespoon ground cumin

1 tablespoon sea salt

2 teaspoons ground allspice

2 teaspoons crushed black pepper

1/2 teaspoon ground chiles

serves 4

Salmon is always better a little pink in the middle. If you cook fish too long, it will become dry and tasteless. To avoid this, sear it on the skin side first at a fairly high heat. The skin will caramelize a little, then when you turn it over you need only brown the flesh side for a short time. Very fast and fresh!

SEARED SALMON
WITH CUCUMBER PICKLE

To make the cucumber pickle, cut the cucumber in half lengthwise, scoop out and discard the seeds, and cut the flesh into 1/2-inch slices. Put the salt, rice vinegar, sugar, chile, and ginger in a bowl, add 1/4 cup water, and mix well. Pour over the cucumber and set aside to marinate.

Brush the salmon fillets with the sesame oil and season with salt and crushed Szechuan pepper. Put the fillets skin side down onto a preheated stove-top grill pan and cook for 4 minutes. Turn the salmon over and cook for a further 1 minute.

Remove from the pan, let rest for a few moments, then serve with the cucumber pickle and a crisp green salad.

4 salmon fillets, 8 oz. each

1 tablespoon toasted sesame oil

sea salt and crushed Szechuan pepper or black pepper

green salad, to serve

cucumber pickle

1 cucumber, about 8 inches long

2 teaspoons salt

1/4 cup rice vinegar

3 tablespoons sugar

1 red chile, seeded and sliced

1 inch fresh ginger, peeled and grated

serves 4

I love to serve this dish whenever I see some really fresh swordfish at the market. It is easy to overcook swordfish, which will become tough, so follow the timings below and err on the side of caution—you can always put the fish back on the heat for a moment or two longer if necessary.

SEARED SWORDFISH
WITH NEW POTATOES, BEANS, AND OLIVES

Brush the swordfish steaks with 1 tablespoon of the oil, season with salt and pepper, and set aside.

To make the dressing, put the remaining oil in a bowl, add the lemon juice, sugar, chives, salt, and pepper, beat well, and set aside.

Cook the potatoes in a saucepan of lightly salted boiling water for 10 minutes, add the beans, and cook for a further 3–4 minutes or until the potatoes and beans are just tender. Drain well, add the olives and half the dressing, and toss well.

Cook the swordfish steaks on a preheated outdoor grill or stove-top grill pan for about 1½ minutes on each side. Let rest in a warm oven for 5 minutes, then serve with the warm potato and bean salad, sprinkled with the remaining dressing and balsamic vinegar.

4 swordfish steaks, 8 oz. each

½ cup extra virgin olive oil

2 tablespoons freshly squeezed lemon juice

½ teaspoon sugar

1 tablespoon chopped fresh chives

1 lb, new potatoes, halved if large

8 oz. string beans, trimmed

2 oz. black olives, such as Niçoise or Kalamata, pitted and chopped, about ½ cup

sea salt and freshly ground black pepper

Reduced Balsamic Vinegar (page 141), to serve

serves 4

POULTRYANDMEAT

I grew up on a farm where we kept hens that were allowed to feed on the grain left behind after the corn had been harvested. They gorged themselves happily on such wonderful food that the benefits to both them and us were obvious to everyone. Now I always buy organic, free range chicken. It is more expensive, but worth every penny.

For many people, duck is probably seen as a bit of a luxury, because it is expensive and sometimes difficult to find. However, it's ideal for cooks short of time, because the breasts cook very quickly. They are sold in many supermarkets, or you can buy a whole duck from the butchers and ask them to cut it into pieces for you (freeze the rest for another time).

When shopping for meat, look for flesh with a good deep color and a layer of fat around it which will keep it moist during cooking. Fat should be creamy in color and almost matt in appearance.

Remember, whatever meat you are cooking, it will need a little time to rest before eating, this lets the meat relax so it is more tender.

Jerk seasoning is Jamaica's popular spice mix, used to spark up meat, poultry, and fish, especially the delicious barbecued offerings sold at the roadside jerk huts so beloved of tourists and locals alike. The seasoning is a combination of allspice, cinnamon, chile, nutmeg, thyme, and sugar and is available in powder or paste form from larger supermarkets and specialty food stores.*

JERK CHICKEN WINGS
WITH AVOCADO SALSA

Put the chicken wings in a ceramic dish. Mix the oil, jerk seasoning, lemon juice, and salt in a bowl, pour over the wings, and stir well to coat. Let marinate overnight.

The next day cook the wings either on a preheated outdoor grill or under a hot broiler for 5–6 minutes on each side, basting occasionally with any remaining marinade until charred and tender.

Meanwhile, to make the salsa, put all the ingredients in a bowl, mix well, and season to taste. Serve the wings with the salsa.

Note If you don't have any jerk seasoning on hand, try another spice mix or spice paste instead. Just remember, jerk is very fiery indeed, so you need a spicy one.

12 chicken wings

2 tablespoons extra virgin olive oil

1 tablespoon jerk seasoning powder or 2 tablespoons paste

freshly squeezed juice of $\frac{1}{2}$ lemon

1 teaspoon sea salt

avocado salsa

1 large ripe avocado

2 ripe tomatoes, peeled, seeded, and chopped

1 garlic clove, crushed

1 small red chile, seeded and chopped

freshly squeezed juice of $\frac{1}{2}$ lemon

2 tablespoons chopped fresh cilantro

1 tablespoon extra virgin olive oil

sea salt and freshly ground black pepper

serves 4

Chinese five-spice powder is a ready-made spice mix used widely in Asian cooking. It is made up of cassia bark (similar to cinnamon), cloves, fennel, star anise, and Szechuan pepper.

ROAST FIVE-SPICE CHICKEN
WITH GINGER BOK CHOY

Wash and dry the chicken pieces and put in a roasting pan.

Put the oil, five-spice powder, ginger, and salt in a bowl, mix well, then brush all over the chicken. Roast in a preheated oven at 400°F for 25 minutes.

Put the honey and soy sauce in a small saucepan and heat until the honey has melted. Stir well, then brush all over the chicken to form a glaze. Return to the oven and roast for a further 10 minutes until the skin is crisp and golden.

To prepare the bok choy, put the soy sauce, chile sauce, and 1/4 cup water in a bowl and mix well.

Heat the two oils in a wok or large skillet, add the ginger, and stir-fry for 30 seconds. Add the bok choy and continue to stir-fry for a further 2 minutes. Add the soy sauce mixture, cover, and simmer gently for 2 minutes, then serve with the chicken.

4 chicken quarters (breasts or legs)

2 tablespoons peanut or safflower oil

1 teaspoon Chinese five-spice powder

1 inch fresh ginger, peeled and grated

1/2 teaspoon salt

3 tablespoons honey

1 1/2 tablespoons dark soy sauce

ginger bok choy

3 tablespoons soy sauce

1 tablespoon sweet chile sauce

2 tablespoons peanut or safflower oil

2 teaspoons sesame oil

1 inch fresh ginger, peeled and finely sliced into matchstick strips

8 small bok choy, halved, well washed, and patted dry with paper towels

serves 4

A great supper dish—simple and quick. Serve it with a green salad, or with this more substantial dish of beans and leeks, which is also very good with lamb. The Mustard and Tarragon Butter is very versatile and goes well with fish such as salmon.

PAN-FRIED CHICKEN
WITH CREAMY BEANS AND LEEKS

To cook the beans and leeks, melt the butter in a saucepan, add the leeks, garlic, and rosemary, and sauté gently for 5 minutes until softened but not golden.

Add the beans, stir once, then pour in the stock. Bring to a boil, cover, and simmer for 15 minutes. Remove the lid, stir in the cream, and add salt and pepper to taste. Simmer, uncovered, for a further 5 minutes until the sauce has thickened. Set aside while you prepare the chicken.

Season the chicken with salt and pepper. Heat the butter and oil in a skillet, and as soon as the butter stops foaming, cook the chicken skin side down for 4 minutes. Turn it over and cook for a further 4 minutes.

Top each breast with a couple of slices of the Mustard and Tarragon Butter and let rest for 2–3 minutes in a warm oven. Serve with the beans and a simple watercress salad.

4 chicken boneless breasts

2 tablespoons unsalted butter

1 tablespoon extra virgin olive oil

1 recipe Mustard and Tarragon Butter (page 140)

sea salt and freshly ground black pepper

watercress salad, to serve

creamy cannellini beans with leeks

4 tablespoons unsalted butter

2 leeks, finely chopped

1 garlic clove, crushed

2 teaspoons chopped fresh rosemary

2 cans cannellini beans, 15 oz. each, about 4 cups, drained, rinsed, and drained again

1 1/4 cups Vegetable Stock (page 143)

1/4 cup heavy cream

sea salt and freshly ground black pepper

serves 4

These mini chickens can be roasted in about 40 minutes. To make sure they are cooked through, push a skewer into the leg meat right down to the bone—if the juices run clear, the bird is cooked. If not, return to the oven for a little longer.

GARLIC-ROASTED CORNISH HENS

Boil the garlic cloves in a saucepan of lightly salted water for 15 minutes, drain, and pat dry (this can be done ahead of time).

Meanwhile, wash the hens, pat them dry, and rub all over with the cut lemon. Chop the lemon into small chunks and put them and the thyme in the body cavities. Season well with salt and pepper and rub the birds all over with 3 tablespoons of the butter.

Put 1 garlic clove in each bird, then put the rest in a large roasting pan. Sit the hens on top and roast in a preheated oven at 400°F for 40 minutes.

Transfer the hens and garlic cloves to a large plate, wrap loosely in aluminum foil, and let rest for 10 minutes.

Meanwhile, to make a gravy, spoon off any excess fat from the roasting pan. Add the wine, bring to a boil, and scrape any sediments into the wine. Boil until reduced by two-thirds. Add the stock and boil for 5 minutes, or until reduced by half. Put the remaining butter and the flour in a bowl and beat until smooth. Gradually beat into the gravy, stirring over gentle heat until thickened.

Serve the Cornish hens with the garlic and gravy.

2 whole heads of garlic, cloves separated but unpeeled

2 Cornish hens

1/2 lemon

4 sprigs of thyme

4 tablespoons unsalted butter, softened

1/2 cup white wine

1 1/4 cups Chicken Stock (page 143)

1 tablespoon all-purpose flour

sea salt and freshly ground black pepper

serves 4

Duck breasts make a quick and easy dish. Cook them in a stove-top grill pan or heavy skillet. The skin will turn very black and crispy from the sugar, and the rich flesh is balanced perfectly by the sweetness of spiced plums.

DUCK WITH SPICED PLUMS

Using a sharp knife, cut several slashes in the duck skin. Rub the skin with salt and pepper. Put the honey and soy sauce in a shallow dish, stir well, add the duck breasts, and let marinate for at least 15 minutes.

Put the vinegar, sugar, cinnamon, and 2 tablespoons water in a saucepan and heat until the sugar dissolves. Bring to a boil, add the plums, and simmer gently for 8–10 minutes until the plums have softened. Let cool.

Meanwhile, heat a stove-top grill pan or heavy skillet until hot, add the duck skin side down, and cook over medium heat for 5 minutes. Turn and cook for a further 4–5 minutes, then remove from the heat and let rest in a low oven for 5 minutes.

Slice the duck crosswise and serve with the plums and a little of the spiced juice.

4 duck breasts, 8 oz. each

1 tablespoon honey

1 tablespoon dark soy sauce

2 tablespoons rice wine vinegar

2 tablespoons palm sugar or soft brown sugar*

1/4 teaspoon ground cinnamon

4 plums, halved and pitted

sea salt and freshly ground black pepper

serves 4

*Palm sugar and other Asian ingredients are available in Chinese stores. If unavailable, use brown or regular sugar.

A simple dish—the Japanese ingredients such as pickled ginger and seven-spice are available in any supermarket selling sushi ingredients. However, go sparingly with the seven-spice pepper—it's a hot little number.

JAPANESE BEEF TATAKI

Brush the meat with the oil and dust very lightly with the seven-spice pepper. Heat a heavy skillet for 5 minutes until very hot, then add the beef and sear on all sides for 2–3 minutes until evenly browned. Remove from the pan and let cool.

Put the dipping sauce ingredients in a bowl, add ¼ cup water, mix well, then divide between 4 small dipping bowls.

Using a very sharp knife, slice the beef thinly and arrange on plates with a little mound of daikon and ginger on each one. Serve with the dipping sauce.

8 oz. beef tenderloin

1 tablespoon peanut or safflower oil

Japanese seven-spice pepper (*shichimi togarashi*)

2-inch piece of daikon (mooli or white radish), peeled and grated

Japanese pickled ginger

dipping sauce

¼ cup Japanese soy sauce (shoyu)

4 teaspoons sake or mirin (sweetened Japanese rice wine)

serves 4

It's important to rest meat for a short time before serving to let it relax and the juices from the steak mingle with the butter. You can serve it with any kind of flavored butter—make up several different kinds, roll them into logs, wrap them in foil, and store them in the freezer to use whenever you need a fast and flavorful addition to a dish. They are good with beef, fish, poultry, and even vegetables.

PAN-FRIED STEAK
WITH HORSERADISH BUTTER

To make the horseradish and chive butter, put the butter, horseradish, and chives in a bowl and beat well. Season to taste with salt and pepper. Form into a log, wrap in foil, and chill for about 30 minutes.

Season the steaks with salt and pepper. Heat the oil in a skillet until very hot and sauté the steaks over medium-high heat for 3 minutes on each side for rare, or a little longer for medium.

Top each steak with 2 slices of the horseradish butter and set aside to rest in a warm oven for 5 minutes, then serve with sautéed potatoes and salad.

4 rib-eye steaks, about 8 oz. each

2 tablespoons extra virgin olive oil

sea salt and freshly ground black pepper

horseradish and chive butter

1¼ sticks unsalted butter, softened

1½ tablespoons grated fresh horseradish

1 tablespoon chopped fresh chives

to serve (optional)

sautéed potatoes

green salad

serves 4

The spices and flavorings used in this recipe are typical of North African cooking, and all over the region, pita bread is stuffed with grilled meat, salad, and yogurt. Use other ground meats if you prefer.

LAMB IN PITA BREAD

Put the coriander and cumin seeds in a small skillet without oil and sauté until they start to brown and release their aroma. Let cool slightly, then grind to powder in a spice grinder (use a clean coffee grinder) or with a mortar and pestle.

Heat the oil in a skillet, add the onion, garlic, and ground spices, and sauté gently for 5 minutes until softened but not golden. Increase the heat, add the lamb and the pinch of salt, and stir-fry for 5–8 minutes until well browned. Stir in the fresh cilantro.

Meanwhile, lightly toast the pita bread and cut a long slit in the side of each one. Carefully fill with a few salad leaves, add the ground lamb mixture, a spoonful of yogurt or tahini, and sprinkle with sesame seeds. Serve hot.

2 teaspoons coriander seeds

1 teaspoon cumin seeds

2 tablespoons extra virgin olive oil

1 onion, finely chopped

2 garlic cloves, crushed

1 teaspoon ground cinnamon

1/4–1/2 teaspoon cayenne pepper

10 oz. ground lamb

a pinch of sea salt

2 tablespoons chopped fresh cilantro

4 pita breads

a few salad leaves, such as romaine lettuce and watercress

plain yogurt or tahini sauce

1 tablespoon white sesame seeds, toasted in a dry skillet

serves 4

Pork can easily become dry. The solution is not to cook it at too high a heat, and in this recipe the sage and prosciutto wrapping help to keep it moist. They have the added advantage of lending more flavor as well. Add the fillets to the pan seam side down so that the prosciutto doesn't unwrap during cooking.

PROSCIUTTO-WRAPPED PORK
WITH SPINACH AND LENTIL SALAD

Cut the pork tenderloins in half crosswise to make 4 servings. Season with salt and pepper. Put 2 slices of prosciutto on a work surface, overlapping them slightly. Add 3 of the sage leaves in a line down the middle. Top with a pork fillet and roll up, keeping the join underneath. Repeat with the remaining fillets.

Heat half the oil in a skillet, add the pork fillets seam side down, and sauté over medium heat for about 12–15 minutes, turning frequently until evenly browned. Transfer to a warm oven and let rest for 5 minutes.

Meanwhile, add the remaining oil to the pan, add the shallots, garlic, and the 1 tablespoon chopped sage, and sauté for 3 minutes until softened but not golden. Add the lentils, chicken stock, and lemon juice and heat through for 2–3 minutes. Stir in the spinach, cook until just wilted, and serve with the pork.

2 pork tenderloins, 12 oz. each

8 thin slices prosciutto

12 large sage leaves, plus
1 tablespoon chopped fresh sage

3 tablespoons extra virgin olive oil

4 shallots, finely chopped

1 garlic clove, crushed

2 cans lentils, 15 oz. each,
about 4 cups, drained,
or 2 cups dried lentils, cooked

1/2 cup Chicken Stock (page 143)

freshly squeezed juice of 1/2 lemon

4 oz. baby spinach leaves

sea salt and freshly ground black pepper

serves 4

The credit for this recipe goes to my mother, who recently served leftover fruit compote (the remains of a crazy day's jam making) with pork chops. It was delicious. Sauté the meat over medium heat so you don't burn the wonderful pan juices, which you then pour over the finished dish.

PORK STEAKS
WITH APPLE AND BLACKBERRY COMPOTE

To make the sauce, put the apples, blackberries, sugar, lemon juice, juniper berries, and 2 tablespoons water in a saucepan. Cover and cook gently until the fruits have softened. Remove the lid and simmer until the juices have evaporated. Remove from the heat, but keep the mixture warm.

Season the chops with salt and pepper. Melt the butter in a large skillet and, as soon as it stops foaming, add the pork. Cook over medium heat for 3–4 minutes on each side until browned and cooked through.

Let rest in a warm oven for 5 minutes. Meanwhile add the sage leaves to the same pan and sauté for a few seconds until crispy. Serve the steaks topped with a spoonful of the compote, the sage leaves, and pan juices.

4 large pork steaks, about 8 oz. each

4 tablespoons unsalted butter

12 large sage leaves

sea salt and freshly ground black pepper

apple and blackberry compote

8 oz. baking apples, cored and cut into thin wedges

²/₃ cup blackberries

2 tablespoons sugar

freshly squeezed juice of ¹/₂ lemon

3 juniper berries

serves 4

Pasta, rice, and noodles play a major role in cuisines around the world—from Asia and India to the Mediterranean and the Middle East, and the rest of the world has adopted them with open arms.

There are many different varieties of rice used in these countries, including basmati in India and Pakistan, sticky rice and black rice in Southeast Asia, the huge number of different rices in Japan, and of course the short-grain Italian rice used in risotto. In most rice-producing countries rice is served at every meal, much as we serve bread in the West. Well, not always!

Noodles are used throughout Asia much as pasta is served in the Mediterranean, and form the basis of many dishes.

These staples provide our main source of carbohydrate and I love them as much for their versatility as their taste. You could cook pasta, noodle, and rice dishes every day of the week without ever feeling bored.

PASTARICENOODLES

Most Asian noodle dishes take just a matter of minutes to cook—in fact, noodles made of rice flour or mung bean starch are ready almost instantly. Wheat-based noodles take the most time—but even then, only about the same as regular dried pasta.

GINGERED CHICKEN NOODLES

Put the rice wine and cornstarch in a bowl and mix well. Cut the chicken into small chunks, add to the bowl, stir well, and set aside to marinate while you prepare the remaining ingredients.

Soak the noodles according to the instructions on the package, then drain and shake dry.

Put all the sauce ingredients in a small bowl and mix well.

Drain the chicken. Heat 1½ tablespoons of the oil in a wok or large skillet, then add the chicken and stir-fry for 2 minutes until golden. Remove to a plate and wipe the pan clean. Add the remaining 1½ tablespoons oil, ginger, and snowpeas and stir-fry for 1 minute. Return the chicken to the pan, then add the noodles and sauce. Heat through for 2 minutes.

Add the garlic chives and cashews, stir well, and serve.

2 tablespoons rice wine, such as Chinese Shaohsing or Japanese mirin

2 teaspoons cornstarch

12 oz. skinless chicken breasts

7 oz. Chinese dried egg noodles

3 tablespoons peanut or safflower oil

1 inch fresh ginger, peeled and thinly sliced

4 oz. snowpeas, finely sliced

¼ cup chopped fresh garlic chives or chives

4 oz. cashews, about 1 cup, toasted in a dry skillet, then chopped

sauce

½ cup Chicken Stock (page 143)

2 tablespoons dark soy sauce

1 tablespoon freshly squeezed lemon juice

1 tablespoon toasted sesame oil

2 teaspoons light brown sugar

serves 4

The instant dashi stock and miso soup stock used in Japanese cooking are available from some larger supermarkets or Asian food stores. Alternatively, use good-quality fresh fish stock.

UDON NOODLES
WITH SEVEN-SPICE SALMON

To cook the noodles, plunge them into a saucepan of boiling water, return to a boil, and simmer for 4 minutes until tender. Drain and refresh under cold water, drain again, and pat dry with paper towels.

Put the dashi or miso stock in a saucepan, add the mirin, soy sauce, tofu, scallions, and wakame, and bring to a boil.

Brush the salmon with the oil and dust with a little seven-spice powder. Put the fillets skin side down on a preheated stove-top grill pan for 4 minutes, then turn and cook for a further 1 minute.

Divide the noodles between 4 deep warmed soup bowls, then add the stock, tofu, and vegetables. Put the salmon on top and serve.

8 oz. dried udon noodles

1½ quarts dashi or miso stock
(see recipe introduction)

¼ cup mirin (sweetened Japanese rice wine) or dry sherry

¼ cup dark soy sauce

4 oz. firm tofu, cut into cubes

6 scallions, trimmed and sliced

a few strands of dried wakame seaweed

4 salmon fillets, 8 oz. each

1 tablespoon safflower or peanut oil

Japanese seven-spice pepper
(shichimi togarashi), (see recipe introduction, page 79)

serves 4

"Tartare" means uncooked and, to serve fish this way, you must use very fresh, sashimi-grade tuna. If you prefer your tuna cooked, sear it on a preheated stove-top grill pan for 1 minute on each side or until cooked to your liking. However, I do urge you to try it tartare.

CHILE TUNA TARTARE PASTA

Cook the pasta according to the instructions on the package.

Meanwhile, heat the oil in a skillet, add the garlic, and sauté gently for 2 minutes until lightly golden. Add the chile, lemon zest, and thyme and sauté for a further 1 minute.

Drain the pasta, reserving $1/4$ cup of the cooking liquid, and return both to the pan. Stir in the hot garlic oil mixture, the lemon juice, the raw tuna, basil leaves, salt, and pepper, and a little extra olive oil. Serve at once.

12 oz. dried fusilli or other pasta

$1/3$ cup extra virgin olive oil

4 garlic cloves, sliced

1–2 dried red chiles, seeded and chopped

grated zest and juice of 1 unwaxed lemon

1 tablespoon chopped fresh thyme leaves

1 lb. tuna steak, chopped

a handful of fresh basil leaves

sea salt and freshly ground black pepper

serves 4

This sauce is best made as soon as the new season's tomatoes arrive in the stores, especially the vine-ripened varieties that we see more and more. If you don't cook with gas, then simply plunge the tomatoes in boiling water for 1 minute, drain, refresh, and peel off the skin.

PASTA WITH FRESH TOMATO

Holding each tomato with tongs or a skewer, char them over a gas flame until the skins blister and start to shrivel. Peel off the skins, chop the flesh, and put in a bowl. Add the oil, chiles, garlic, basil, sugar, salt, and pepper and leave to infuse while you cook the pasta (or longer if possible).

Cook the pasta according to the instructions on the package. Drain well and immediately stir in the fresh tomato sauce. Serve at once with the grated cheese.

2 lb. ripe tomatoes

1/3 cup extra virgin olive oil

2 fresh red chiles, seeded and chopped

2 garlic cloves, crushed

a bunch of fresh basil, chopped

1 teaspoon sugar

12 oz. dried spaghetti

sea salt and freshly ground black pepper

freshly grated pecorino or Parmesan cheese, to serve

serves 4

Pasta is the archetypal fast food. This one is fast and fresh, with the ricotta melting into the hot pasta and coating it like a creamy sauce. The pine nuts give it crunch, while the herbs lend a fresh, scented flavor. If you don't have all the herbs listed here, use just arugula plus one other—the parsley or basil suggested, or perhaps chives, snipped with shears.

PASTA WITH MELTED RICOTTA
AND HERBY PARMESAN SAUCE

Cook the pasta according to the instructions on the package.

Meanwhile, heat the olive oil in a skillet, add the pine nuts, and sauté gently until golden. Set aside.

Drain the cooked pasta, reserving 1/4 cup of the cooking liquid, and return both to the pan. Add the pine nuts and their olive oil, the herbs, ricotta, half the Parmesan, and plenty of cracked black pepper. Stir until evenly coated.

Serve in warmed bowls, with the remaining cheese sprinkled on top.

12 oz. dried penne or other pasta

1/3 cup extra virgin olive oil

1 cup pine nuts, about 4 oz.

4 oz. arugula, thinly sliced

2 tablespoons chopped fresh parsley

2 tablespoons chopped fresh basil

8 oz. fresh ricotta cheese, about 1 cup, mashed

4 oz. freshly grated Parmesan cheese, about 1 1/4 cups

cracked black pepper

serves 4

SHRIMP FRIED RICE

Heat the oil in a wok and swirl to coat. Add the garlic, ginger, and chile and stir-fry for 30 seconds. Add the shrimp, peas, scallions, and dried shrimp and stir-fry for 2 minutes until the shrimp turn pink.

Using a spatula, push the mixture to one side, add the eggs, and scramble until set. Then add the rice and stir over a high heat for 2 minutes until heated through.

Stir in the soy sauce, lemon juice, and cilantro and serve.

Note Asian dried shrimp are available in packages in Chinese markets. They keep very well in an airtight container if you don't use all of them.

2 tablespoons peanut or safflower oil

2 garlic cloves, chopped

1 inch fresh ginger, peeled and grated

1 fresh red chile, seeded and chopped

12 oz. small uncooked shrimp, peeled, deveined, and coarsely chopped

10 oz. frozen peas, about 2 cups, thawed

6 scallions, trimmed and sliced

1/4 cup Asian dried shrimp*

2 eggs, lightly beaten

5 cups cooked jasmine rice
(from 1 3/4 cups uncooked rice)

3 tablespoons light soy sauce

freshly squeezed juice of 1/2 lemon

2 tablespoons chopped fresh cilantro

serves 4

COCONUT AND LIME LEAF RICE

Put the rice in a strainer and wash under cold running water until the water runs clear. Drain and shake well.

Put the rice, coconut milk, lime leaves, lemongrass, and salt, and 1 1/2 cups water in a heavy saucepan. Bring to a boil, cover with a tight-fitting lid, and simmer very gently for 20 minutes.

Remove the pan from the heat but leave undisturbed for a further 10 minutes. Fluff up with a fork and serve.

2 cups jasmine rice

1 1/2 cups coconut milk

12 lime leaves, bruised, or grated zest of 2 unwaxed limes

1 stalk of lemongrass, bruised

1 teaspoon sea salt

serves 6

Adding a nip of vodka right at the end adds a delightful flavor to this risotto. Although this recipe takes slightly longer than most in the book, it is simple to make and always a terrific success with guests.

FENNEL AND LEMON RISOTTO

Soak the saffron in the hot stock until required. Finely chop the fennel and the fronds.

Melt half the butter in a skillet, add the onion, chopped fennel, garlic, and lemon zest, and sauté gently for 10 minutes until softened. Add the rice and stir for 30 seconds until the grains are glossy.

Meanwhile, heat the saffron stock to a gentle simmer. Add a ladle of the stock to the rice and cook, stirring until absorbed. Continue adding the stock a little at a time, stirring, and cook for about 20 minutes until the liquid is absorbed and the rice is *al dente* (just done).

Remove the pan from the heat, stir in remaining butter, lemon juice, vodka, Parmesan, reserved fennel fronds, salt, and pepper, cover, leave for 5 minutes, then serve.

a small pinch of saffron threads

5 cups hot Vegetable Stock (page 143)

1 large fennel bulb

1¼ sticks unsalted butter

1 onion, chopped

2 garlic cloves

juice and grated zest of
1 unwaxed lemon

1½ cups risotto rice, such as arborio

½ cup vodka

¼ cup freshly grated Parmesan cheese

sea salt and freshly ground black pepper

serves 4

PIZZA AND BREAD

By their very nature, pastry, pizza, and bread doughs take time, but I did want to have some in the book. I love making them and there are many delicious breads that are relatively fast.

Making dough for pizzas is deceptive—although you should allow time for the dough to rise, the actual preparation and cooking time is short. I often make up a batch of dough, then go out to do the rest of the shopping. You can even leave it in a coolish place for the day, then punch it down just before baking. I have included three different pizza recipes and, if time is limited, you can use a package pizza dough mix or a frozen pizza base as an alternative.

The two bread recipes use dough that doesn't need to rise, drastically reducing the preparation time. The soda bread is a timeless classic, great served with soup and is also delicious toasted. The cornbread is spiked with chile and cilantro. It is wonderfully savory, can be eaten warm, and is also great toasted.

If you are really short of time you can cheat a little here and use a 16 oz. pack of frozen dough, cut in half—for two people you will need a whole package. Follow the instructions on the pack but let the dough rise for 15 minutes after you've rolled it out.

MOZZARELLA PIZZA
WITH GARLIC AND ROSEMARY

To make the dough, sift the flour into the bowl of a food mixer fitted with a dough hook attachment or a food processor fitted with a plastic blade. Add the yeast and salt, then work in the oil and water to form a soft dough.

Remove from the bowl and transfer to a floured work surface. Roll into a ball, and put in an oiled bowl. Cover with plastic wrap and let rise for about 45 minutes or until doubled in size.

Preheat the oven to its highest setting, about 500°F and put a pizza stone or baking tray on the top shelf to heat.

Divide the risen dough in half and transfer one half to a well-floured surface. Roll it out to 12 inches diameter. Take the hot stone or baking tray from the oven and carefully put the pizza base on top. Spread with half the mozzarella, garlic, and rosemary leaves, then season with salt and pepper and sprinkle with a little extra oil. Bake in the preheated oven for 10–12 minutes until bubbling and lightly golden. Repeat with the second pizza.

It is best to eat the pizzas as soon as they come out of the oven, so I recommend sharing each one as they are cooked.

1²⁄₃ cups all-purpose flour, plus extra for dusting

1 teaspoon active dry yeast (½ a packet)

1 teaspoon sea salt

1 tablespoon extra virgin olive oil, plus extra to serve

½–²⁄₃ cup very warm water

topping

8 oz. fresh mozzarella cheese, chopped

2 garlic cloves, sliced

2 sprigs of rosemary

sea salt and freshly ground black pepper

a pizza stone or baking tray

serves 2–4

If you are making fresh pizza bases, I recommend that you cook the pizzas one at a time and eat them as soon as they are ready (unless you have two ovens). Use the regular rather than convection setting on your oven to make sure that you have a good, crisp base on the pizza.

TOMATO PIZZA
WITH CAPERS AND ANCHOVIES

If using pizza base mix, prepare the dough according to the directions on the package. Put the dough in a bowl and let rise until doubled in size.

Preheat the oven to its highest setting, about 500°F, and put a pizza stone or baking tray on the top shelf to heat.

Divide the risen dough in half and transfer one half to a well-floured surface. Roll it out to 12 inches diameter. Take the hot stone or baking tray from the oven and carefully put the pizza base on top. Add half the tomatoes, capers, anchovies, mozzarella, and a few basil leaves. Bake in the preheated oven for 10–12 minutes until bubbling and golden. Serve at once, then repeat to make a second pizza.

1 recipe Pizza Dough (page 107),
2 packs pizza base mix (6½ oz. each),
or 1 pack frozen pizza dough
(16 oz.), halved

all-purpose flour, for dusting

2 large ripe tomatoes, chopped

2 tablespoons capers,
rinsed and drained

12 anchovy fillets in oil,
drained and chopped

8 oz. fresh mozzarella cheese, chopped

a few basil leaves

sea salt and freshly ground black pepper

a pizza stone or baking tray

serves 2

Not a pizza, not a tart, but halfway between the two, and totally delicious. Usually, a pizza is cooked on a preheated pizza stone so that the base will be crisp. You can use a preheated baking tray to achieve a good result.

MUSHROOM MASCARPONE PIZZA

If using pizza base mix, prepare the dough according to the directions on the package. Transfer the dough to a bowl and let rise until doubled in size.

Preheat the oven to its highest setting, about 500°F, and put a pizza stone or baking tray on the top shelf to heat.

Heat the oil in a skillet and sauté the garlic and thyme for 1 minute. Add the mushrooms and sauté for a further 4–5 minutes until they are brown but haven't started to release their juices. Season with salt and pepper.

Divide the risen dough in half and transfer one half to a well-floured surface. Roll it out to 12 inches diameter. Take the hot pizza stone or baking tray from the oven and carefully put the pizza base on top. Spoon half the mushrooms on top and dot with half the mascarpone.

Sprinkle with half the Parmesan and bake in the preheated oven for 10–12 minutes until bubbling and golden. Serve at once and then repeat to make a second pizza.

1 recipe Pizza Dough (page 107), 2 packs pizza base mix (6½ oz. each), or 1 pack frozen pizza dough (16 oz.), halved

6 tablespoons extra virgin olive oil

2 garlic cloves, sliced

1 tablespoon chopped fresh thyme

1 lb. small cremini mushrooms, sliced

all-purpose flour, for dusting

8 oz. mascarpone cheese

⅓ cup freshly grated Parmesan cheese, about 1 oz.

sea salt and freshly ground black pepper

a pizza stone or baking tray

serves 2–4

The classic Irish soda bread is made with baking soda as the raising agent rather than yeast. This means the dough can be baked immediately, rather than having to let it rise as with a yeasted dough. Quick and easy to make.

SODA BREAD

Put the flour, baking soda, salt, and sugar in a bowl and mix well. Make a well in the center, add the buttermilk, and gradually work it into the flour to make a soft dough.

Knead on a lightly floured surface for 5 minutes and then shape into a flattened round loaf. Transfer to an oiled baking tray and, using a sharp knife, cut a cross in the top of the dough. Sprinkle with a little extra flour.

Bake in a preheated oven 450°F for 15 minutes, then reduce the heat to 400°F and bake for a further 30 minutes until risen and the loaf sounds hollow when tapped underneath.

Transfer to a wire rack and let cool completely.

$2^2/_3$ cups whole wheat flour, plus extra for dusting and sprinkling

1 teaspoon baking soda

1 teaspoon sea salt

1 teaspoon sugar

$1^1/_4$ cups buttermilk

a baking tray, oiled

makes 1 small loaf

I like to cook this cornbread in a deep loaf pan so later it can be sliced and toasted more easily. However, if you are short of time, pour the mixture into a greased baking pan lined on the bottom with parchment paper and cook for 20–25 minutes.

CHILE CORNBREAD

Sift the flour and baking powder into a bowl and stir in the cornmeal and salt.

Mix the eggs, buttermilk, and oil in a second bowl, then, using a wooden spoon, stir into the dry ingredients to make a smooth batter. Stir in the corn, chile, and cilantro and pour into the prepared loaf tin.

Bake in a preheated oven at 400°F for 40 minutes. Let cool in the pan for 5 minutes, then remove from the pan and let cool on a wire rack.

$1/2$ cup all-purpose flour

1 tablespoon baking powder

$1^1/3$ cups medium cornmeal or polenta

1 teaspoon sea salt

3 eggs, beaten

$1^1/4$ cups buttermilk

$1/4$ cup extra virgin olive oil

8 oz. canned corn kernels, about 1 cup, drained

1–2 fresh red chiles, seeded and chopped

2 tablespoons chopped fresh cilantro

a deep loaf pan, 2 lb., greased and bottom lined with parchment paper

serves 8–12

As a child I remember every main meal ended with a dessert, but today this seems to be something most of us reserve for a dinner party or at best the weekends. Time and health issues may well be the reason for this, but not all sweet things have to be rich and heavy, and some don't take long to prepare. Good-quality fresh fruit needs little to adorn it—just pick flavors that work well together and combine them simply.

If your sweet tooth is utterly incorrigible, you will probably decide that chocolate is worth whatever time it takes, so I have included some drinks and desserts for you. Other "proper desserts" take a little more time, but are worth every second, I'm sure you'll agree.

Fast & Fresh wouldn't be complete without a section on drinks and, although many drinks are already quick and simple to prepare (only a few seconds to open that chilled bottle of wine), I'm always on the lookout for new combinations—James Bondi is one of my favorites, now that I live in Sydney.

DESSERTSANDDRINKS

Strawberries and black pepper are surprisingly good partners. The orange flower water adds a lovely perfumed quality to the strawberries, but can be omitted.

STRAWBERRIES WITH BLACK PEPPER

Hull the strawberries and cut in half. Sprinkle with the orange flower water, if using, and with the sugar, and black pepper. Chill for 15 minutes and serve.

Note Strawberries should be washed and dried before hulling, not after, otherwise they fill up with water.

1 lb. strawberries

1 tablespoon orange flower water (optional)

1 tablespoon sugar

2 teaspoons cracked black pepper

serves 4

RHUBARB COMPOTE WITH YOGURT

Rose water, like orange flower water, is sold in the baking section of supermarkets, in drugstores, and in ethnic food stores specializing in Middle Eastern or Indian products.

Cut the rhubarb into 2-inch slices and put in a saucepan. Add the sugar and ¼ cup water. Bring to a boil, cover, and simmer gently for 15 minutes until the rhubarb has softened. Taste and stir in extra sugar if necessary. Transfer to a dish and let cool.

Put the yogurt, honey, and rose water in a bowl, mix well, then serve with the rhubarb.

1 lb. rhubarb, trimmed

¼ cup sugar, or to taste

½ cup plain yogurt

1 tablespoon honey

½ tablespoon rose water

serves 4

Vanilla sugar is easy to make—just put a couple vanilla beans in a bottle of sugar and leave them there, topping up with fresh sugar as necessary. You can use the beans for cooking, pat dry with paper towels, then return to the sugar. If you don't have vanilla sugar, use regular sugar and a drop of vanilla extract.

ROASTED PEACHES

Cut the peaches in half, remove the pits, and arrange the fruit cut side up in a roasting pan. Pour over the honey and roast in a preheated oven at 400°F for about 20 minutes until softened and lightly golden.

Mix the mascarpone with the vanilla sugar and lemon juice and spoon onto the hot peaches. Serve at once.

4 large ripe peaches

2 tablespoons honey

8 oz. mascarpone cheese, 1 cup

3 tablespoons vanilla sugar

1 tablespoon freshly squeezed lemon juice

serves 4

Melon and ginger are a classic combination of flavors, and this simple version is perfect for a warm summer's day. You can use any type of melon, but my favorite is cantaloupe.

MELON WITH GINGER SYRUP

Put the sugar and $2/3$ cup water in a small saucepan and heat gently to dissolve the sugar. Bring to a boil, add the ginger and lemon juice, and simmer gently for 3 minutes. Remove from the heat and let cool.

Cut the melon into wedges, scoop out the seeds, and serve sprinkled with ginger syrup.

$1/3$ cup sugar

1 inch fresh ginger, peeled and finely chopped

freshly squeezed juice of $1/2$ large lemon

1 large ripe melon

serves 4–6

Fruit fritters are delicious and very simple to make. I serve them with cinnamon ice cream, available in some supermarkets and gourmet food stores. Cinnamon and banana make an excellent flavor combination, but choose your own favorite flavor.

BANANA FRITTERS
WITH CINNAMON ICE CREAM

Peel the bananas, cut into 4 chunks, then cut the chunks in half lengthwise.

To make the batter, sift the flour and salt in a bowl, beat in the egg yolk, ginger beer or sparkling water, and oil to form a smooth batter. Beat the egg white in a separate bowl until soft peaks form, then fold into the batter.

Heat 2 inches of the oil in deep saucepan until it reaches 350°F or until a cube of bread turns golden brown in 30 seconds.

Dip the banana chunks into the batter and deep-fry in batches of 3–4 for about 1 minute until the batter is crisp and golden. Drain on paper towels and keep the fritters warm in a moderate oven while you cook the remainder. Serve with a scoop of cinnamon ice cream.

2 large bananas

cinnamon ice cream, to serve

ginger batter

1/3 cup all-purpose flour

a pinch of sea salt

1 egg, separated

1/3 cup ginger beer or sparkling water

1 tablespoon peanut or safflower oil, plus extra for deep-frying

serves 4

Bread and butter pudding was one of my childhood favorites, and I couldn't have been happier than when it enjoyed a revival a couple of years ago. This is my version of this wonderful retro recipe, and if you make them in individual dishes, they will cook in under 20 minutes.

BREAD AND BUTTER PUDDINGS

Put the milk, cream, vanilla, and 3 tablespoons of the sugar in a saucepan and heat until the sugar dissolves.

Put the eggs in a bowl, beat well, stir in 2–3 tablespoons of the hot milk mixture to warm the eggs, then stir in the remainder of the hot milk.

Lightly toast the slices of brioche and cut into quarters. Divide between the 6 prepared ramekins and sprinkle with the raisins.

Pour in the custard, grate a little nutmeg over the top, then sprinkle with the remaining tablespoon of sugar. Bake in a preheated oven at 350°F for 18–20 minutes until firm. Remove from the oven, let cool a little, then serve warm.

1¼ cups milk

1¼ cups heavy cream

½ teaspoon vanilla extract

¼ cup sugar

3 eggs

6 thick slices of brioche bread or hot cross buns, about 8 oz., halved

2 oz. golden raisins, ⅓ cup

1 whole nutmeg

6 ramekins, 1 cup each, well buttered

serves 6

Even if you never make desserts at any other time, you probably do when you have people to dinner. Perfect for a dinner party, these little plum fudge desserts can be prepared well ahead of time, then cooked just before serving.

PLUM FUDGE DESSERTS

Put the butter, honey, and cream in a saucepan and heat until melted. Put the sugar, spice, and bread crumbs in a bowl and stir well.

Divide half the butter-honey mixture between the ramekins and top with a layer of plum slices and half the bread crumb mix. Add the remaining plums and bread crumbs, then spoon over the remaining butter-honey mixture.

Set on a baking tray and bake in a preheated oven at 400°F for 20 minutes. Remove from the oven and let cool for 5 minutes, then carefully unmold the desserts and serve with a spoonful of sour cream or crème fraîche.

4 tablespoons unsalted butter

4–5 tablespoons honey

2 tablespoons heavy cream

2 tablespoons brown sugar

1 teaspoon apple pie spice
or a pinch of cinnamon plus a little
freshly grated nutmeg

1½ cups fresh white bread crumbs

2 ripe plums, halved, pitted, and
thinly sliced

sour cream or crème fraîche, to serve

4 ramekins, ⅔ cup each

serves 4

Chocolate and rosemary may sound an unusual combination, but in fact the flavors go very well together. Remove the mousses from the refrigerator about 1 hour before serving so that they can return to room temperature.

CHOCOLATE AND ROSEMARY POTS

Put the cream and rosemary sprigs in a saucepan and heat slowly just to boiling point. Remove from the heat and leave to infuse for 20 minutes.

Strain into a clean pan, add the chocolate, and heat very gently until the chocolate melts—don't let the mixture boil. Remove from the heat, let cool slightly, then stir in the egg yolks one at a time. Finally add the butter, stirring until melted.

Pour the mixture into the espresso cups and let cool. Chill for 2 hours. Spear each chocolate pot with a rosemary sprig, if using, just before serving.

$1\frac{1}{4}$ cups light cream or half-and-half

2 sprigs of rosemary, bruised, plus 6 extra, to serve (optional)

8 oz. bittersweet chocolate, chopped

2 egg yolks

2 tablespoons unsalted butter

6 espresso cups or small ramekins

serves 6

Brownies are everyone's favorite chocolate indulgence. They're not complicated to make, but the better the chocolate, the better they will be. The most important rule is to aim for the right texture—just set on top, but wonderfully gooey and melting on the inside. Most people can't resist eating them the minute they come out of the oven—plain or with a cup of coffee. But if you can wait, try them as a quick dessert, with cream or ice cream, or with a cup of coffee.

CHOCOLATE AND CINNAMON BROWNIES

Put the hazelnuts in a dry skillet and toast over medium heat until aromatic. Do not let burn. Let cool, then chop coarsely.

Put the chocolate and butter in a heatproof bowl set over a saucepan of simmering water and melt gently. Put the eggs and sugar in a bowl and beat until pale. Stir in the melted chocolate, flour, cinnamon, white chocolate chips, and chopped hazelnuts.

Spoon into the prepared pan and bake in a preheated oven at 375°F for 30–35 minutes until the top sets but the mixture still feels soft underneath.

Remove from the oven and let cool in the pan. Serve cut into squares.

1/2 cup blanched hazelnuts, about 3 oz.

10 oz. bittersweet chocolate

2 1/4 sticks unsalted butter

3 eggs

1 cup plus 2 tablespoons sugar

1/2 cup self-rising flour

2 teaspoons ground cinnamon

3 oz. white chocolate chips

a baking pan, 9 x 13 inches, greased and bottom lined with parchment paper

serves 8–12

These pastry puffs filled with chocolate remind me of the delicious French pastry, *pain au chocolat*. Making them with frozen puff pastry dough is even faster than a trip to the pâtisserie. If you prefer, you can use plain dark chocolate instead of the white.

SPICED WHITE CHOCOLATE PUFFS

Put the puff pastry dough on a floured work surface and cut each sheet into 4 pieces, 4 inches square.

Put 3 pieces of chocolate onto each square, then add a light dusting of apple pie spice (I use a small tea strainer). Dampen the edges with a little water, then fold them over diagonally to form a triangle. Press the edges together to seal, then, using the blade of a sharp knife, gently tap the sealed edges several times (this will help the pastry rise).

Transfer the triangles to the baking tray. Put the egg yolk and milk in a small bowl, beat well, then brush over the dough. Bake in a preheated oven at 425°F for 10–15 minutes until risen and golden.

Remove from the oven, let cool for 5 minutes, lightly dust with cocoa powder, and serve.

2 sheets ready-rolled puff pastry dough, thawed if frozen

all-purpose flour, for dusting

8 oz. white chocolate, cut into 24 squares

1 teaspoon apple pie spice
or a pinch of cinnamon plus a little freshly grated nutmeg

1 egg yolk

2 tablespoons milk

unsweetened cocoa powder, to serve

a baking tray, greased

makes 8

The perfect nightcap, sleepytime chocolate with a hint of romantic after-dinner mints—just the thing to send you off into a peaceful sleep, or warm you up on a chilly winter's afternoon.

MINTED HOT CHOCOLATE

Put the milk and mint sprigs in a saucepan and heat very gently until boiling. Boil for 1 minute, then remove from the heat. Discard the mint.

Divide the chocolate between 2 mugs. Stir in the milk and continue to stir until melted. Serve the sugar separately, if using.

2¾ cups milk

4 sprigs of fresh mint, bruised lightly to extract flavor

2 oz. bittersweet chocolate, chopped

sugar, to taste (optional)

serves 2

Kids will love this shake, particularly with a spoonful of extra ice cream. I've made it optional, but of course it can't possibly be!

CHOCOLATE AND BANANA CINNAMON SHAKE

Peel and chop the bananas. Put the ice cream, bananas, milk, and cinnamon in a blender and purée until smooth. Pour into tall glasses and serve with an extra scoop of chocolate ice cream, if using.

2 bananas

4 scoops chocolate ice cream, plus extra to serve (optional)

1¼ cups milk

1 teaspoon ground cinnamon

serves 4

Tisane is the French word for an infusion of herbs, flowers, or other aromatics. I think it's a beautiful word for this deliciously spicy drink, which I've chilled down to make a great contrast between hot and cold.

CHILLED LEMONGRASS TISANE

Put the chile in a heatproof bowl with the lemongrass, ginger, and sugar, then add 1 quart boiling water and the lemon juice, and stir to dissolve the sugar. Set aside to infuse until room temperature.

Strain the cooled liquid and chill for at least 30 minutes, then serve in tall glasses with mint leaves and ice cubes.

1–2 fresh red chiles, seeded and sliced

2–4 stalks of lemongrass, outer leaves discarded, inner section finely sliced

2 inches fresh ginger, peeled and sliced

¼ cup sugar

freshly squeezed juice of 2 lemons

mint leaves and ice cubes, to serve

serves 4

My juicer has a citrus attachment as well as a juicer, so this drink couldn't be simpler. If you don't have the citrus press, just peel the oranges and put them through the regular juicer (don't forget to remove all the bitter white pith).

ORANGE AND APPLE REFRESHER

Push the oranges, apples, and ginger through the juicer. Half-fill 2 tall glasses with ice cubes, pour the juice over the top, and serve.

2 large oranges, peeled

2 Granny Smith apples

1 inch fresh ginger, peeled

ice cubes, to serve

a juicing machine

serves 2

JAMES BONDI

A variation on the classic champagne cocktail I found at a funky Sydney bar, beside the famous beach that inspired the pun.

Put the sugar lumps in 6 champagne flutes, add the vodka, and stir with a spoon until the sugar completely dissolves (crush it slightly if necessary).

Add a dash of bitters to each one, top up with champagne, and serve.

6 brown sugar lumps

1/4 cup vodka

a dash of Angostura bitters

1 bottle chilled champagne

serves 6

CAMPARI GRAPEFRUIT SLUSH

2 3/4 cups ice cubes

1/4 cup Campari

3/4 cup ruby grapefruit juice

sugar, to taste

serves 4

Campari and grapefruit juice are a marriage made in heaven, lovely with or without sugar.

Put the ice cubes in a blender and grind until crushed. Add the Campari and grapefruit juice and blend until slushy. Add sugar to taste. Serve in chilled glasses with short cocktail straws.

PEACH SANGRIA

A white wine variation of the more classic Spanish aperitif, cool and delightful on a hot summer's day.

Pour the wine in a large pitcher, then add the peach liqueur, sliced peaches, orange, and lemon. Add ice cubes and stir well. When ready to serve, half-fill tall glasses with ice cubes, wine, and fruit, then top up with the lemonade.

1 bottle chilled dry white wine

1/4 cup peach liqueur

4 large ripe peaches, sliced

1 orange, sliced

1 unwaxed lemon, sliced

ice cubes

chilled lemonade

serves 6

THE BASICS: FLAVORED OILS, BUTTERS, AND DRESSINGS

OILS Herbs, spices, and aromatics can all be added to oils to enhance the flavor and provide another valuable staple for the pantry. They should be infused in the oil for about 7 days for the best results. Heating the oil and flavorings over a gentle heat speeds up the process as well as killing off any harmful bacteria. It is always best to strain the oil after the flavors have developed, then store in a cool place.

Another method of flavoring oil is to purée the herb and oil, then strain off the residue. This gives a vibrant green oil with a lovely flavor. As well as recipes for Fragrant Garlic Oil (page 21), Basil Oil (page 26), here are:

Thyme Oil

6 sprigs of fresh thyme

2¾ cups extra virgin olive oil

makes 2¾ cups

Lightly tap the thyme sprigs with a rolling pin to help release the aromas and put in a screw-top bottle. Add the oil and leave to infuse for at least 7 days. Strain into a clean bottle and use as required.

Chile Oil

1¼ cups extra virgin olive oil

4 dried red chiles, coarsely chopped

makes 1¼ cups

Put the oil and chiles in a screw-top bottle and leave to infuse for 2 days before using.

BUTTERS Flavoring butter with spices and herbs is great fun as well as cost effective—just think of the amount of herbs you throw away when you have chopped up a few too many. There are so many different combinations of flavors you can use. Try Horseradish and Chive (page 80), or one of the following:

Mustard and Tarragon Butter

2 tablespoons chopped fresh tarragon leaves

1 tablespoon whole grain mustard

1¼ sticks unsalted butter, softened

makes 4 oz.

Beat the tarragon and mustard into the butter. Roll into a small log, wrap in plastic wrap, and freeze until required.

Cilantro, Lime, and Pepper Butter

2 tablespoons chopped fresh cilantro

1¼ sticks unsalted butter, softened

grated zest and juice of 1 unwaxed lime

½ teaspoon cracked black pepper

makes 4 oz.

Finely chop the cilantro, then beat into the butter with the remaining ingredients. Roll, wrap, and freeze, as above.

Mint and Cumin Butter

Although this is a great partner for lamb chops, I also like it tossed with cooked baby new potatoes and left for a few minutes to infuse.

½ tablespoon cumin seeds

2 tablespoons chopped fresh mint

1¼ sticks unsalted butter, softened

makes 4 oz.

Toast the cumin seeds in a dry skillet for about 3 minutes until they start to "pop" and release their aromas. Cool, then crush with a mortar and pestle.

Finely chop the mint leaves and beat into the butter with the cumin seeds. Roll, wrap, and freeze, as above.

DRESSINGS I always like to keep a jar of homemade dressing in the refrigerator so that making a salad for lunch takes just a few minutes. If the dressing includes herbs, it is best made just before you use it—or make up the dressing, but leave the herbs until the last minute. You'll find other dressing recipes throughout the book—Lemon and Cilantro (page 55), Black Bean (page 31), and others—but here are some of my favorites:

Classic French Dressing

2/3 cup extra virgin olive oil

2 tablespoons white wine vinegar

2 teaspoons Dijon mustard

1/2 teaspoon sugar

sea salt and freshly ground black pepper

makes 3/4 cup

Put all the ingredients into screw-top bottle and shake until amalgamated. Store in the refrigerator and shake again before using.

Salmoriglio

This Italian dressing is served with broiled fish or chicken—I love it with red mullet or bream. Look out for the sweet Italian-style lemons now more widely available.

3/4 cup extra virgin olive oil

freshly squeezed juice of 1 large lemon

2 tablespoons chopped fresh parsley

2 garlic cloves, crushed

a pinch of dried oregano

sea salt and freshly ground black pepper

makes 1 cup

Put all the ingredients into a screw-top bottle and shake well. Serve the same day.

Reduced Balsamic Vinegar

Reducing a cheap balsamic vinegar produces a sauce almost as good as an aged balsamic, which would cost a great deal more. It may seem like a terrible waste simply to boil away the vinegar but the resulting thick glaze can be used sparingly and will provide a delicious finish to many dishes.

1 1/4 cups balsamic vinegar

makes 1/2 cup

Put the vinegar in a small saucepan and boil gently until it is reduced by two-thirds and reaches the consistency of thick syrup. Let cool, then store in a clean bottle.

SAUCES AND STOCKS

SAUCES Many useful sauces appear throughout this book. Others include:

Mayonnaise

Some extra virgin olive oils can make this sauce slightly bitter, so I use a gentler oil such as French or Spanish. You can also use a mixture of extra virgin and pure olive oils.

2 egg yolks

2 teaspoons white wine vinegar or lemon juice

1/4 teaspoon salt

2 teaspoons Dijon mustard

1 1/4 cups extra virgin olive oil

freshly ground black pepper

makes about 1 1/4 cups

Put the egg yolks, vinegar or lemon juice, salt, and mustard in a food processor and blend briefly until frothy. With the blade running drizzle the oil in through the funnel until the sauce is thick and glossy. It may be necessary to thin the mayonnaise slightly by blending in 1–2 tablespoons boiling water. Season to taste. To store in the refrigerator for up to 5 days, cover the surface with plastic wrap.

Quick Tomato Sauce

A simple, quick, delicious sauce to be tossed through pasta, spread over a pizza base, or used as the base for a chicken or bean stew.

2 cans chopped tomatoes (16 oz. each)

4 garlic cloves, crushed

1/4 cup extra virgin olive oil

1 teaspoon sugar

1 teaspoon dried oregano

2 tablespoons chopped fresh basil

sea salt and freshly ground black pepper

serves 4–6

Put the tomatoes, garlic, oil, sugar, oregano, salt, and pepper in a saucepan. Bring to a boil, and simmer, covered, over gentle heat for 30 minutes until reduced and well flavored.

Stir in the basil, and salt and pepper to taste. Serve, or cool and refrigerate overnight.

Quick Romesco Sauce

The traditional method for this Catalan sauce includes a dried red pepper, rather than paprika.

2 oz. blanched almonds

3 garlic cloves, chopped

1/3 cup extra virgin olive oil

2 ripe tomatoes, coarsely chopped

2 tablespoons red wine vinegar

2 teaspoons smoked paprika

1 teaspoon sugar

1/2–1 teaspoon chili powder

sea salt

makes 1 1/4 cups

Put the almonds in a dry skillet and sauté over medium heat until browned. Cool, then transfer to a food processor, add the garlic, and blend briefly until coarsely ground.

Add the remaining ingredients, purée until fairly smooth, then season to taste. Store in the refrigerator for up to 3 days.

Almond and Parsley Pesto

This variation of regular basil pesto can be tossed through pasta, served with chicken or even used as a dip for bread.

2 oz. blanched almonds, about 1/2 cup

1 oz. pine nuts, about 1/4 cup

a large bunch of flat-leaf parsley

2 garlic cloves, chopped

3/4 cup extra virgin olive oil

2 tablespoons freshly grated Parmesan cheese

sea salt and freshly ground black pepper

makes about 1 1/4 cups

Put the almonds in a dry skillet and sauté over medium heat until browned, transfer to a bowl. Repeat with the pine nuts and let cool.

Put the nuts in a food processor, add the parsley and garlic, and blend briefly. Add the oil and purée until smooth and vibrantly green. Stir in the cheese and season to taste. Store in the refrigerator for up to 5 days.

STOCKS Though recipes in this book are fast and fresh, I include recipes for three basic stocks—make them when you have time and freeze them for later. You can also buy fresh stocks, but if you use stock cubes, look for the organic type, which have better flavor.

Vegetable Stock

2 onions, chopped

2 potatoes, chopped

2 leeks, sliced

4 carrots, sliced

1 large celery stalk, sliced

4 tomatoes, chopped

6 oz. mushrooms, chopped

4 garlic cloves, chopped

1/4 cup rice or green lentils

2/3 cup dry white wine

4 sprigs of parsley

2 sprigs of thyme

2 teaspoons sea salt

1 teaspoon black pepper

makes about 6 cups

Put all the ingredients in a saucepan and add 7 cups water. Bring to a boil, cover, and simmer for 1 hour.

Pour through a fine stainer and taste. Reduce the stock by simmering gently to enhance the flavor. Refrigerate up to 3 days or freeze for up to 3 months.

Chicken Stock

2 lb. chicken backs and wings

2 carrots, coarsely chopped

3 celery stalks, coarsely chopped

1 onion, chopped

1 leek, chopped

6 garlic cloves, chopped

2 tomatoes, coarsely chopped

2 fresh bay leaves

2 sprigs of fresh thyme

6 white peppercorns

1 teaspoon salt

makes about 6 cups

Put all the ingredients in a saucepan and cover with about 2 quarts water. Bring to a boil, skim off the foam, and simmer gently, uncovered, for 1 hour.

Pour through a fine strainer and let cool completely. Refrigerate until required or freeze for up to 3 months.

Fish Stock

2 lb. fish frames

4 cups dry white wine

2 carrots, coarsely chopped

2 celery stalks, coarsely chopped

1 onion, chopped

1 leek, sliced

1 garlic clove, chopped

2 fresh bay leaves

2 sprigs of parsley

6 white peppercorns

1 teaspoon salt

makes about 4 cups

Wash the fish trimmings and put in a large saucepan with all the remaining ingredients. Add 2 quarts water, bring to a boil, skim off the foam, and simmer gently for 30 minutes.

Strain in a clean pan and simmer until the stock is reduced to about 4 cups. Let cool completely and refrigerate until required or freeze for up to 3 months.

INDEX

144

CONVERSION CHART

Weights and measures have been rounded up or down slightly to make measuring easier.

volume equivalents

American	Metric	Imperial
1 teaspoon	5 ml	
1 tablespoon	15 ml	
1/4 cup	60 ml	2 fl. oz.
1/3 cup	75 ml	2½ fl. oz.
1/2 cup	125 ml	4 fl. oz.
2/3 cup	150 ml	5 fl. oz. (1/4 pint)
3/4 cup	175 ml	6 fl. oz.
1 cup	250 ml	8 fl. oz.

weight equivalents

Imperial	Metric
1 oz.	25 g
2 oz.	50 g
3 oz.	75 g
4 oz.	125 g
5 oz.	150 g
6 oz.	175 g
7 oz.	200 g
8 oz. (1/2 lb.)	250 g
9 oz.	275 g
10 oz.	300 g
11 oz.	325 g
12 oz.	375 g
13 oz.	400 g
14 oz.	425 g
15 oz.	475 g
16 oz. (1 lb.)	500 g
2 1b.	1 kg

measurements

Inches	Cm
1/4 inch	5 mm
1/2 inch	1 cm
3/4 inch	1.5 cm
1 inch	2.5 cm
2 inches	5 cm
3 inches	7 cm
4 inches	10 cm
5 inches	12 cm
6 inches	15 cm
7 inches	18 cm
8 inches	20 cm
9 inches	23 cm
10 inches	25 cm
11 inches	28 cm
12 inches	30 cm

oven temperatures

110°C	(225°F)	Gas 1/4
120°C	(250°F)	Gas 1/2
140°C	(275°F)	Gas 1
150°C	(300°F)	Gas 2
160°C	(325°F)	Gas 3
180°C	(350°F)	Gas 4
190°C	(375°F)	Gas 5
200°C	(400°F)	Gas 6
220°C	(425°F)	Gas 7
230°C	(450°F)	Gas 8
240°C	(475°F)	Gas 9